KILLER TENNIS

JOHN R. POWERS AND CAROL KLEIMAN

Illustrations by

GARY PATTERSON

A THOUGHT FACTORY BOOK

CONTEMPORARY
BOOKS, INC.
CHICAGO

Library of Congress Cataloging in Publication Data

Powers, John R.
  Killer tennis.

  1. Tennis—Anecdotes, facetiae, satire, etc.
  I. Kleiman, Carol.   II. Title.
GV996.P64   1985   796.342'0207   85-4224
ISBN 0-8092-5255-4

Published by Contemporary Books, Inc.
180 North Michigan Avenue, Chicago, Illinois 60601
Manufactured in the United States of America
Library of Congress Catalog Card Number: 85-4224
International Standard Book Number: 0-8092-5255-4

Published simultaneously in Canada by Beaverbooks, Ltd.
195 Allstate Parkway, Valleywood Business Park
Markham, Ontario L3R 4T8 Canada

Published by arrangement with the Thought Factory
P.O. Box 5515, Sherman Oaks, CA 91413

To Jim Kraiss, Reverend Victor Rudden, and Richard Snyder—three of the nicest Killers I know.

John R. Powers

To my loyal Killer Tennis Partner, Larry Townsend, and to our equally loyal Killer Opponents, Sherry Goodman and Dick Watt.

Carol Kleiman

CONTENTS

1

FORTY-L~~OV~~E HATE

Tennis. "It's only a game." Right. And breathing is only a hobby. Have you ever noticed that the person who says, "Tennis is only a game," is always the one who's winning it?

Face it. Tennis is not fun. It was never meant to be. Look at the pros on television. Do they remind you more of a warm puppy or of a Doberman on a short leash? Regardless of what you hear or say, in tennis, as in life, there is only one point—destroying your opponent.

If you think you have to become a better player in order to be a winner in tennis, then this book is not for you. As Dear Abby would say, "Wise up, Dearie." Good tennis players concentrate on such trivial matters as their serve, return of serve, ground strokes, and their net game. Killer Tennis Players concentrate on the only thing that counts, the score. Remember, "Sneak softly and carry a big, a very big, racket."

WINNING IS EVERYTHING

KILLER'S ROW:
CASE NO. 69855370

Sally Goshkin, champion of the Glenwood Park District Tennis Tournament, shown here with her three children, "Net Ball," "Backspin," and "Out-by-an-Inch."

2

COURTING YOUR VICTIM

A mistake many tennis players make is that they actually like their opponents. In an ideal world, you and your opponent would enter the court from opposite sides, tear each other's hearts out for several sets, and then go your separate ways. But, alas, this is not a perfect world. What happens is that most of us end up playing tennis against people we like. Disgusting.

Although you try to avoid it, inevitably you end up learning the other person's name. You gradually discover what your opponents do for a living, the names of their kids, their hopes, their dreams, and other meaningless drivel. Before you know it, you begin thinking of your opponent as . . . a . . . well, for lack of a better word, a human being. And a decent one at that. Come on. You know better. Decent human beings don't play tennis.

In order to understand better the weaknesses of that mass of flesh standing at the opposite end of the court, it would be wise to trace the various routes their lives have taken that have led them to that last stop of degeneracy: Playing tennis with you.

1. **The Traditionalist**. The rest of us grew up playing baseball in the street, hopscotch on the sidewalk, doctor behind the house, and waited for either our wedding day or a job on the ice cream truck so we could wear white. At the same time, however, the Traditionalist was on the tennis court at the country club, behaving like the back end of the polo pony while learning the proper strokes. The Traditionalist believes that the game should be played on grass (yes, the game of tennis), but clay courts are acceptable. Traditionalists play only with wooden rackets. They consider metal rackets tacky and oversized rackets downright immoral. Killer Tennis Players, on the other hand, would, if strength allowed, hit their forehands with a garage door. For the Traditionalist, tennis is a social game. Killers realize that there is no such thing. Social diseases, yes, but not social tennis. Traditionalists don't mind losing as long as they look good doing it.

THE TRADITIONALIST IN READY POSITION

2. **The Professional Amateur Athlete**. For these individuals, tennis is just another sports stop on the way to the cemetery. They played touch football until their knees no longer worked and basketball until their lungs no longer worked. Now, they'll play tennis until their brains no longer work. After they put down their rackets, about the only thing they'll be good for is golf. The Professional Amateur Athletes don't mind losing as long as they get "plenty of exercise." In tennis, losers always get a lot of exercise. They don't notice that the only time a Killer Tennis Player moves more than five feet is at the end of the match when he or she goes to the net to shake the loser's hand.

THE PROFESSIONAL AMATEUR ATHLETE

3. **Frumps,** so named because of the sound they make when they run into each other, which they frequently do. Frumps are the ones who show up on a public tennis court once every two or three years wearing Bermuda shorts, black socks, street shoes, and baseball caps worn sideways. They tend to travel in herds like Jersey cows, although Jersey cows look considerably brighter. Frumps often bring along their young children, sandwiches, and even blankets. Not surprising that Frumps cannot tell the difference between a beach and a tennis court. Four or five of them will attempt to play at the same time using only three rackets among them. Their shots are like their lives—40 yards out of bounds.

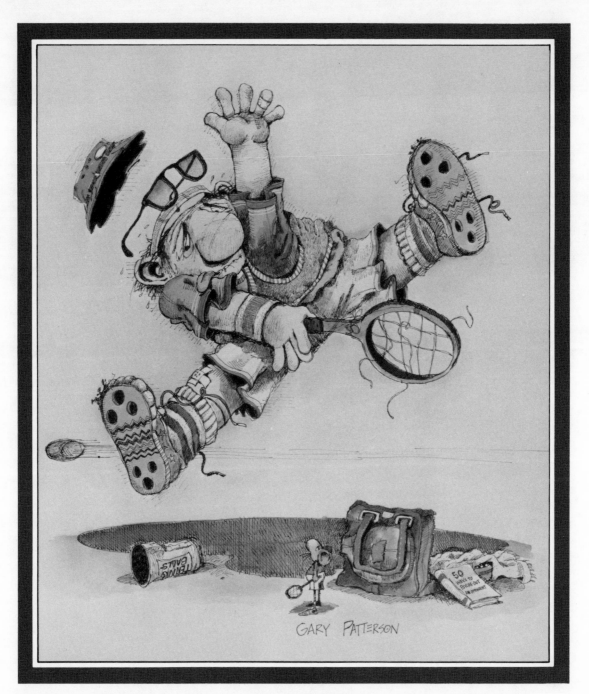

THE FRUMP

Killer Tennis Players are a little like all three of the above. They're Traditionalists. What better tradition than wiping out your opponent? Like the Professional Amateur Athletes, Killer Tennis Players' brains are working just fine. Killers are even a little like Frumps. Every now and then, they, too, will hit a ball 40 yards out of bounds. The only difference is, a Killer will claim it's in.

THE KILLER

3

DRESSED
TO KILL

As every alligator knows, clothes don't make the tennis player. But even Killers do their business better when they're well dressed.

Warm-up suits are the perfect thing to wear if you've just gained 1,200 pounds, like to loiter in discount stores, or can't afford pajamas. They can even be worn while you warm up for tennis.

Avoid designer labels or opponents will begin to think you have enough money to pay for your half of the court.

Although white is the traditional color for tennis wear, Killer Tennis Players, like militant blacks, kissed off whites a long time ago. Losers allow fashion, tradition, or sales to determine what they wear on a tennis court. But Killer Tennis Players find out what they're playing in front of and dress accordingly. To them, it's one of life's mysteries why a chameleon has never won the Grand Slam. If, for instance, you are playing in front of a green tarp, army fatigues would be the perfect outfit. You can, however, dress too well. Bill and Heather Wherearethey once lost an important doubles match by default. No one knew they were there.

If you'd like to wear a variety of tennis colors but you can't because of a limited budget, then do start out by buying basic whites. Just wear them long enough and they will become a variety of colors.

KILLER'S ROW:
CASE NO. 66666666

Dr. O. Wotta Sliceberg, born at the Almost Inn, February 29. Developer of the most popular serve in tennis today: the Leap Year Serve—it goes in once every four years.

4

DEATH GRIPS

Other tennis books will tell you that there are a number of ways to grip a racket, such as the Western, the Continental, and the Eastern grips. But Killer Tennis Players know that there's only one way to grip a racket: the Death Grip.

The Death Grip is murderous when used for the basic strokes: the forehand, backhand, serve, volley, lob, smash, slam, bludgeon, maul . . . .

THE DEATH GRIP

With the Death Grip, you never shake hands with the racket. Instead, you immediately slap it across the face and punch it in the head. You then put your hands on the throat of the racket, imagine that it's your opponent's throat, and twist. Then place both hands on the racket handle as if it were an ax and begin swinging at your opponent.

If the Death Grip doesn't immediately destroy your opponent, don't panic. Get a grip on yourself. Doing so won't help your tennis game, but it'll get your mind off it. Killers have to have a little fun, too.

KILLER'S ROW:
CASE NO. 8029847928473

Killer Tennis Player Lawrence Long-Wind Noenda was on his daily four-mile run when he spotted a tennis ball in the curb. Lawrence was not only long-winded but also frugal. He picked up the ball and went to put it in his pocket when he realized that he didn't have any pockets because he was wearing running shorts. So he just stuck the ball under the band of his shorts and continued running.

About a half hour later, he was standing in front of his house cooling down when a neighbor walked by. They got into a conversation, but every now and then, he noticed her glancing down. Finally, Lawrence glanced down.

"Oh," he said, remembering, "that's a tennis ball."

Said his neighbor: "I know what you're going through. Last year, my husband had tennis elbow."

5

PUTTING THE HEAT ON

The best way to become a Killer Tennis Player is to commit many little murders in the warm-up. Properly done, you will finish the warm-up "warm" and "up," while your opponent will remain dead cold. The moment you get on the court, throw yourself on the ground and begin doing push-ups. It's impressive if you use only one arm. It's even more impressive if you use none. Continue doing push-ups until your opponent finishes opening the can of balls. (Killers don't do things that make disgusting sounds.)

WARMING UP

When your opponent is ready to warm up, spin your racket in your hand a few times and study it closely. Tap the strings and casually mention that your new racket is experimental, cost over $5,000, was developed by the Pentagon, and that you are legally required to register it with the police.

As you begin hitting the ball with your opponent, find out what he or she doesn't like and do it. If he likes to hit hard, hit soft. If she wants to practice coming to the net, lob. Whenever your opponent's balls hit the white line or crawl over the net, remind him he's using up all his luck. Look bored. Never give him your full attention. Carry on a conversation with other tennis players—who are four courts down—read a book, go shopping.

At the end of the warm-up, mention to your opponent, "I'm really glad we're playing today. I'm coming back from an injury, and you know how important it is to start back slowly."

KILLER'S ROW:
CASE NO. 501288265

Tennis pro Lou Capelli, nicknamed "The Pope" because he is Catholic, Italian, and always wears a white dress.

THE POPE

6

"STOP ME BEFORE I SERVE AGAIN"

The serve is the most important part of tennis. In order to serve well, one must possess strength, dexterity, brilliant eye and hand coordination, and tremendous mental discipline. In short, talent. Killer Tennis Players are many things—vicious, mean, petty, spiteful, despicable. But talented? Killer Tennis Players realize that it's not so important that you actually serve the ball well, but that you look like you're serving the ball well. Like every other area of life, create a lot of motion and people are going to presume that you're doing something important.

The Motion: Losers worry about tossing the ball straight into the air, meeting it with the racket at the precise instant of its highest ascent, and then following through to the sounds of Beethoven's Ninth Symphony. Killers, however, know that the only rule worth remembering is that in serving the ball you make the same motion as if you were throwing your racket. Since it is the same motion, Killers just take aim and throw their rackets. Then they toss the ball into the service area for an easy ace. Your opponent will find it very difficult to return the serve when he or she has been knocked unconscious.

The Grunt: The critical moment of the serve is the grunt. Like most good things in life, a great grunt depends on an active fantasy. For instance, just as you're about to hit the ball, imagine that your car is stuck in a 10-foot snow drift and you have to push it out. Orson Welles is behind the wheel—at least most of him is. Sitting next to him are John Candy and Mahalia Jackson. In the back seat is the Mormon Tabernacle Choir. And everybody you know is on your back. Grunt! When great grunters get too old to play tennis, they often get jobs as the sound tracks in porno movies.

FIRST SERVE

Timing: Also a vital element of a good serve. Your racket should be meeting the ball, and your weight should be shifting forward at the precise moment your opponent has left the court for a drink of water.

Footwork: As any pro will tell you, if your feet are in the right place, then so is your tennis game. Killers know that great footwork will always save them from a humiliating defeat. You watch your opponent warm up by hitting serves so fast that the human eye can barely perceive them as they skim through the service box. But it's no contest when you show off your fancy footwork . . . by walking off the court.

The Second Serve: Killer Tennis Players just love second serves. Like the rest of the spineless slobs who make up the world, Killers also just dink it in, at least for the first few games. But Killers immediately realize when their opponent begins playing a sneaky game of "Red Light, Green Light." Every time a Killer taps in that second serve, the opponent sneaks up another few inches. Within a few games, the opponent has succeeded in pressing his or her head right up against the barrel of the gun and a Killer Tennis Player is more than delighted to pull the trigger. On the next second serve, the Killer sends over a torpedo disguised as a tennis ball. With decent luck, the Killer will have succeeded in putting the ball right through the opponent's head. Quite honestly, though, such a wound may or may not affect an opponent's future play. After all, every tennis player has one or why else would he or she be involved in the game?

SECOND SERVE

7

SIZING UP YOUR OPPONENTS AND THEN CUTTING THEM DOWN TO SIZE

Killers look at their opponents and then play the killing game accordingly. If, for instance, your opponent is grossly overweight, every time he or she serves, yell "Foot Fault." Who's to know?

If there's a big difference in speed between you and your opponent, make sure you bring the balls. If he or she is slow-footed, bring championship balls . . . as long as they were used in a championship that was played before 1950. If your opponent's faster, then pump the balls with helium. Not only will the balls bounce higher, giving you a few more moments to get there, but if you inhale the helium, you'll sound like Donald Duck. It's very difficult to play good tennis against anyone who sounds like Donald Duck . . . unless you're Daffy.

KILLER'S ROW:
CASE NO. 773127584

On September 3, 1975, Martha Marvelous posted a major coup for women's lib by defeating Macho Mahusky, 6-0, 6-0. At the time, unfortunately, they were playing doubles and he was her partner . . .

8

A KILLER CALLS

One of the truly beautiful things about tennis is that, if played properly, you can draw blood from your opponent on almost every play. In other words, you get to referee your own game.

You should always presume that your opponent is a highly moral, fair-minded individual who would never even think of cheating—someone who will consistently give you the close calls. Most importantly, remember that this kind of person naturally thinks that you're just like him or her. Killer Tennis Players know a lamb when they see one.

HOW A KILLER CALLS

1. Never call a ball "Long" or "Wide," although if your opponent hits one into the net, it is certainly acceptable to yell, "Short." When you say, "Long," or "Wide," you are helping your opponents to adjust their next shot. Other acceptable comments are "You've got to be kidding" and "What a great shot . . . for doubles." On a particularly close call, the first thing you should say to your opponent is "Did you see it?" When your opponent makes an absolutely brilliant shot, call it out before the ball even leaves the racket.

2. Nonverbal signals are also acceptable ways of informing your opponent of his or her inadequacies. On a particularly crucial point, hold up two fingers to indicate that the ball missed by less than an eighth of an inch. Putting your finger down your throat indicates that your opponent missed by considerably more than that. The index finger is the universally accepted signal for an "out" ball. Another finger can be used to indicate an "in" ball.

CALLING THE SHOT

3. Just as important as making calls is your reaction to your opponent's calls. When you hit a ball three feet out of bounds and your opponent calls it that way, give him or her a long stare followed by a muttered "You owe me one." Other physical reactions can include a big sigh, chuckles, a slight shake of the head, turning your back on him or her for a few hours, and gun shots.

4. When a Killer's opponent spins his or her racket and asks a Killer to call it, a Killer says, "Handle," takes the balls and heads for the base line.

KILLER'S ROW:
CASE NO. 887564213

Two tennis players, whose minds had both double-faulted, were sitting in the state mental home.

"Tomorrow," announced the one, "I, John McEnroe, will play in my fifth Wimbledon Championship. My strategy is to hit nothing but topspins to the backhand. When I win, I'll be considered the greatest tennis player of all time."

"Well, John," said the other fellow, "If I were you .. and, incidentally, I am . . ."

9

Mug Shots

Profiles of Killer Tennis Players are closely guarded secrets, withheld from public view by the CIA, the USTA, and Interpol. But when you sneak a look at their files—and Killer Tennis Players *are* sneaks— you learn more than you'll ever want to know about the nature of the beast.

Criminal tennis records are kept according to the profession of the Killer. And, unlike the score of a match, not even Killer Tennis Players can change them, fix them, make them up as they go along, or pay someone from the old neighborhood to "take care" of them.

The only way Killer Tennis Players can change these descriptions of themselves is to get a new job, and who would want to hire them after seeing their records? Who would want to hire them anyway?

PROFESSIONAL KILLER TENNIS PLAYERS' PROFILES

Stock Market Analysts: When they're ahead by two points, they split.

Psychiatrists: Play for 50 minutes and walk off the court.

Executives: Blame all their mistakes on their secretaries.

Accountants: Keep trying to balance their rackets.

Secretaries:	**Make 80 shots a minute while answering phones, taking dictation, and going out for coffee at the same time.**
Salespeople:	**Play 12 hours a day and get no benefits.**
Doctors:	**Always wear white, and when they come to the net and give you a shot, they charge $25 a visit.**
Waiters and Waitresses:	**When you ask them the score, they say it's not their court.**

KILLER SECRETARY

10

DOUBLE JEOPARDY

As far as Killer Tennis Players are concerned, doubles are just singles with somebody in the way. For Killers, the real problem with doubles is that you don't always get the credit you deserve. For instance, if your opponents are rushing to the back of the court to hit a lob and you yell, "Look out for the Pontiac!" your partner might get credit for it.

KILLER DOUBLES

There are only three good reasons for playing doubles:

1. The only way you and your opponent can get a tennis court is to play doubles with two dopes who already have one.

2. You are proud of the fact that there are at least three people in the world who can stand the sight of you for as long as a tennis match.

3. You're over 130 years old and you can't move more than three feet in a month.

There are time-tested ways to endear yourself to your doubles partners so that whenever they hear the term *double fault* they will always think of you:

1. When you're at the net and your partner is serving, announce that you're going back to the baseline on the second serve because "Up there, I haven't got a chance."

2. After this remark, when your partner inevitably double-faults, shake your head, sigh, and give that look you normally reserve for mistakes you step in.

3. Casually mention to your partners that the other team is trying to hit all the balls to them.

4. When you're at the net and someone hits one down the alley on you, even though your partner is at the far end of the court, yell, "Yours!"

5. Give your partner lessons as you go along.

6. At least once, say, "Well, that was my mistake," implying that the other two thousand were your partner's.

7. At the first opportunity after a set, offer to switch partners.

TEAMWORK

Mixed Doubles: This involves playing tennis with the weaker sex. Unless you can agree on exactly which one that is, you have no business playing mixed doubles.

KILLER'S ROW:
CASE NO. 5709386217293

Donald "The Dink" Durban, who fatally wounded many an opponent by waiting for just the right moment to dink the ball over the net. Died suddenly when his most recent opponent "dinked" him on the head with a crowbar.

THE DINK

11

DEALING WITH THE JOINT

Killer Tennis Players love injuries—not their own, of course. There is, according to Killers, only one healthy approach to tennis injuries: Cause them.

Because they're built so strangely, Killer Tennis Players themselves are immune to bodily hurts. After all, their Achilles' heel is their ego, and they can't stomach their hearts.

12

KILLERS AND KIDS

Killer Tennis Players don't play tennis with kids. In tennis, kids are either disgustingly good or simply disgusting. Kids themselves cannot be Killer Tennis Players— grape juice cannot be wine.

13

PSYCHO TENNIS

Killer Tennis Players know that in order to play winning tennis it's not so important how fast your legs run but rather how well your mouth runs.

WHEN TO SAY IT:	WHAT TO SAY:
You're changing sides.	I think I lost my contact lens, so if you hear a crunch, that's 200 bucks.
Your opponent bounces the ball 18 times before serving it.	Either pick up the damn jacks or serve it.
Your opponent misses on the first attempt to serve.	First fault.
The ball is just in.	Just out.

WHEN TO SAY IT:	WHAT TO SAY:
You've just hit a ball 80 yards out of bounds.	When did the wind stop?
Your opponent is about to serve for a crucial point.	Wait a sec. I have to tie my shoes . . . the pair at home.
You've just missed an incredibly easy point.	(Holding up your racket) Hey, this thing's got holes in it.
Your opponent has just made a great serve.	What a rotten return.
You're one game away from wrapping up the set and your opponent starts a winning streak.	Don't worry about the time. I can visit my old, sick mother another night . . . possibly.
Your opponent has apparently suffered a heart attack.	Hey, I didn't know we were playing Sudden Death.

14

Conning the Pro

After a while, all tennis players need professional help. Unfortunately, they usually go to a tennis pro. The tennis pros who hang around park districts and indoor courts are not Killer Tennis Players. If they were, they'd either be in Wimbledon or in jail. But because of their undisputed knowledge of traditional tennis, they *can* help a Killer in that most important stroke of all: looking good.

Pick a pro who can teach you how to bounce balls up from the court with just your racket. This move intimidates your opponent because it's so professional. Minimally, you should learn how to pick up the ball with your racket and the side of your foot. It's highly amateurish to end up with your shoe in your hand.

Devote your next lesson to learning exactly how to play a Sudden Death tie. That way, the next time you're in a tied set, you can announce to your opponent that you alone understand the rules for such a situation and proceed to cheat to your heart's content.

Other cons you can learn from your pro are: how to open a can of balls while losing less than three fingers and how to run around your backhand without break dancing.

THE TENNIS PRO

15
CORPORAL PUNISHMENT SERVES THEM RIGHT

In doubles, as in singles, players take turns serving. In Killer Tennis, doubles partners let the stronger server—if there is one—serve every game.

If your opponents complain, ask them, "What do you want us to do—lose?

KILLER'S ROW:
CASE NO. 4757389222

Tennis Pro Sammie, the Smoothie, Sellem, who claimed he was all ready to serve and was clocked at over 90 miles an hour. Unfortunately, he was in bed at the time.

16

Highway ROBBERY

Singles means one person playing another, but if you are losing a match, Killer Tennis Players should feel free to call in someone extra for temporary help.

Usually the most efficient assistance can be had from one or two professional football players or from one or two IRS auditors who share your side of the net.

When you get ahead by two sets—and you will—ask the temporary help to leave the court because you "want to finish this easy one off by myself."

17

TAKE THIS QUIZ— OR ELSE!

ARE YOU A KILLER TENNIS PLAYER?

	TRUE	FALSE
1. Killer Tennis Players practice against the wall—by running into it.	☐	☐
2. Killer Tennis Players never say, "Nice try," except to murder suspects.	☐	☐
3. Killers never join expensive clubs—but always play at them.	☐	☐

KILLER PRACTICE

	TRUE	FALSE
4. Killers believe there should be capital punishment for people who say, "What's the score? I've been having so much fun I can't remember."	☐	☐
5. Killers love to see little children, hardly as tall as their rackets, running around the court chasing balls—through their gun sights.	☐	☐
6. Killer Tennis Players respect human life, but not as much as an overhead.	☐	☐

THE OVERHEAD SMASH

		TRUE	FALSE

7. When you hit your ball onto Killer Tennis Players' court, they don't wait until they finish their point to toss it back to you . . . they don't toss it back to you.   ☐   ☐

8. Killer Tennis Players hit the ball right at you so you don't have to run for it—especially when they're only three inches away.   ☐   ☐

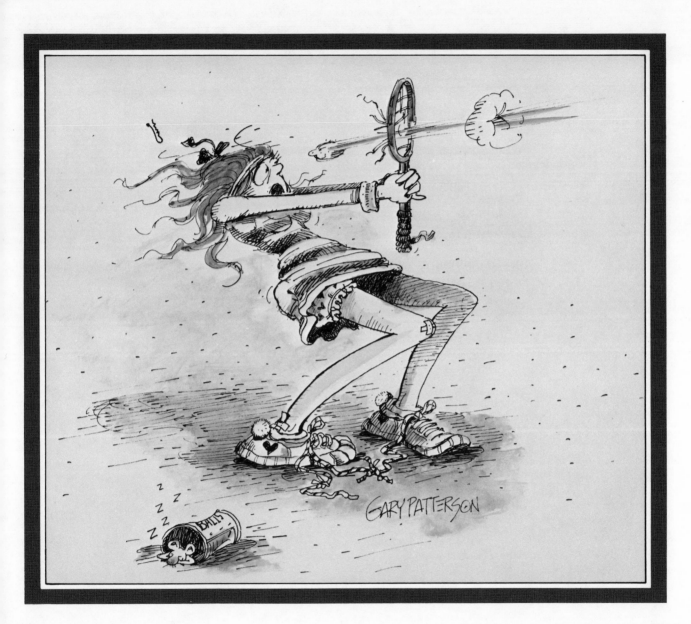

	TRUE	FALSE
9. Killer Tennis Players don't talk about business on the court—they tend to it.	☐	☐
10. To determine who serves first, Killers don't spin their rackets. They spin their opponents.	☐	☐

SPINNING FOR SERVE

HOW TO FIGURE OUT
YOUR SCORE

Don't bother, wimp. Killer Tennis Players
don't waste their time on quizzes.

KILLER'S ROW:
CASE NO. 263548375968

Killer California Cool Conway, the first player to be disqualified from Wimbledon for snorting the baseline.

18

KILLERS MAY LOSE, BUT NEVER THEIR APPEAL

Even when a Killer Tennis Player loses, he or she has the gift of being able to cut the heart out of the joy of their opponent. Killers are adept at postponing the inevitable. After losing the third set, a Killer is quick to yell, "Come on, haven't you ever heard of a seven set match?"

Another Killer reaction to losing is snidely replying to your opponent, "Remember what Vince Lombardi said, "Winning isn't everything." (No one ever said you had to remember every word Lombardi said.)

Killers also know that when your smug opponent leaps over the net to shake your hand, that's an excellent time to practice your serve for your next big match.

SPORTSMANSHIP

19

THE PERFECT CRIME

The one rule that Killer Tennis Players must keep in mind that will absolutely, positively guarantee they will never, never, ever lose in tennis:

PICK THE RIGHT OPPONENT

THE PERFECT OPPONENT

20

BECOME AN OFFICIAL KILLER TENNIS PLAYER

It pays to advertise. Even Killers know that. As an extra source of intimidation, we are offering a Killer Tennis T-shirt. Such a shirt is easily worth one game per set . . . unless your opponent is also wearing one. Better buy two.

All you have to do is send $10 (plus $1.50 in handling costs) to:

Killer Tennis
P.O. Box 5515
Sherman Oaks, CA 91413

Sizes are, "Murder 1" (extra large), "Man Slaughter" (large), "Reckless Homicide" (medium), and "Oops" (small).